Creating Your BE-Print™

DRAFTING YOUR

PERSONAL

BLUEPRINT

FOR LIVING

Shelley Roy
Glenn Smith

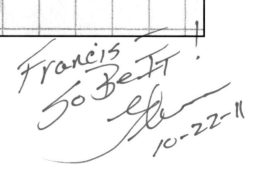

Francis —
So Be It!
Glenn
10-22-11

This book is dedicated to our families — Kelli Bedenbaugh-Smith, Mattson Taylor Smith, Karlie Brooke Smith, Wesley Gordon Roy, and Duncan Thomas Roy — who for the past five years have been immersed in the journey of the creation of the BE-Print System. They have been our test subjects, our sounding boards, our examples in teaching, our supporters, our advisors, and our greatest advocates. Each in his or her own ways has held us accountable to being the person we have told them we wanted to be. May they know that they have ignited within each of us a bundle of potential for which we will be eternally grateful!

Creating Your BE-Print: Drafting Your Personal Blueprint for Living
© 2010. Shelley A.W. Roy and Glenn Smith
Published by Five Crows Publishing

Book design by Kelly Prelipp Lojk

ISBN: 978-0-9844314-0-3

Acknowledgements

The ideas in this book would not exist without the support of our colleagues, teachers, mentors, and past workshop participants. Colleagues at the International Association of Applied Control Theory have shared their thinking, successes, and expertise to help us grow both personally and professionally. Special thanks to William T. Powers, our teacher and mentor, for his theory of human behavior: Perceptual Control Theory. In addition, our understanding of PCT has benefited greatly from our association with the dedicated professionals at The Control Systems Group. We would also like to acknowledge the contributions of our past workshop participants. Their willingness to help us test the BE-Print™ waters have greatly benefited the program's development and our ability to help others help themselves. Kudos to our awesome editor, Kelly Prelipp Lojk, who finds a way to read our minds, capture our thinking, and put it into words that sound just like us. Our sincere gratitude goes to George Hallak, whose words and deeds have championed our passion for these ideas and our work.

Contents

Testing the Waters

> *"There is no point forcing learning on anyone who is not ready to swim in its waters."*
>
> Tom Butler-Bowdon

*W*e believe there is a reason this book is in your hands at this moment. Perhaps you were intrigued by the title. Maybe someone you admire recommended the book to you. On the other hand, you may know one or both of us and wanted to see what we've been up to for the past eight years. There is of course the possibility that you are a self-help junkie and are always on the lookout for something more to read about the final frontier... the depths inside of you. Whatever the reason, we want to take some time for you to dip your toe into the waters of what we have to offer, making sure you are ready to swim. We promise to try not to throw you into the deep end right away, and we hope to give you ample time along the way to simply float and enjoy. We know that some of you may be afraid of the deep waters of self-evaluation. If this is you, take it slow, one small step at a time. Stick your toe in and when that's comfortable, perhaps your whole foot. No one but your inner voice will be looking over your shoulder judging your bravery. Some say that that little voice in your head is not your conscience, but your ego. Let go of your ego and enjoy the water. Confronting our fears brings the greatest joy in the end. If you feel yourself going under, call for help by visiting us online at www.BE-Print.net. There we will give you some ideas for putting on a life preserver so you can relax in these new waters for a while or head to shore by setting the book aside and coming back when you are ready. Whatever works for you in this exploration of **you** — recognize it, savor it, remember it, and learn from it.

For over thirty years now, we have been helping people help themselves to become the people they want to be. We have challenged individuals, groups, and organizations to look within to find the answers that will move them in the direction they wish to go. We have challenged them, not with our beliefs, but with *their own* beliefs. That is what this book is all about: having you look deep within to explore the depths of **you**! This may be uncharted territory. What makes this approach to exploration different is its strong foundation in scientific research on human behavior — Perceptual Control Theory (PCT) along with the latest thinking on learning, change, leadership, and organizational development. We are both self-proclaimed knowledge junkies, and we both know that by synthesizing these bodies of research we can better address a broader audience of learners.

When we began this journey we did not know each other. We lived in different parts of the country and came from different yet similar fields of study, Glenn from psychology and Shelley from education. We did have several things in common: our compassion for all living systems, our desire to give back, and our insatiable thirst for the continuous growth of mind, body, and spirit. When we met near the end of the twentieth century, we both were involved with exploring the work of William Glasser and William T. Powers. Shelley, being the more technical-oriented, was very involved with understanding the theoretical underpinnings and research supporting PCT, while Glenn was more involved in exploring and experimenting with the implementation of the ideas. We both valued the practicality of these ideas and saw the importance of using them when working with the individuals and organizations we served.

There are three things that make this book different from most self-help books.

- Everything we do today is based on our understanding of PCT, a scientific theory of human behavior and motivation that crosses all cultures.

- The focus of this book is on this moment forward. We believe in living in the now with our eye on the future. Every great swimmer knows that you keep looking at where you are going, not at where you have been. And if you get tired, you tread water and stay put. The only time we will ask you to open the door to your past is to find strategies that have worked for you. We also encourage you to recognize those things that haven't worked in the past and pull those lessons into your present situation. *It is only your frustration over your past that is an issue in the present.*

■ In this book, we will be consciously focusing on the positive aspects of your present and future. We know that many programs and counselors believe you must first heal old wounds before you can try to overcome them. That's not us. We will ask you to engage in self-evaluation and self-reflection, trying to pull from within you the person you want to be. Remember, we hope to challenge your beliefs not with *our* beliefs but with *your own* beliefs. This means you need to take time to figure out what you believe. We did not come to this with a specific picture of what "normal" is or what a "good" person is. Nor do we believe we have the answers for you. Based on PCT, we believe that we are most effective when we help others find the answers within themselves.

We encourage you to make notes in this book or grab a blank journal to take along your journey. Simply reading the exercises will not give you the full benefit of practicing the exercises. Both the process and the product are important. With several of these exercises, you may find you need to come back to them and revise or rethink them. You may want to use a pencil, not a pen.

This is not a one-time process; this is a lifetime process. Creating a habit of self-evaluation requires discipline. We will be asking you to see where in your life you are already self-disciplined and how you might transfer some of those skills and strategies to creating and living your BE-Print. As your life's journey continues you may find what was a priority five years ago is a non-issue today. Our beliefs, desires, and priorities change over time. We will encourage you to keep revisiting your BE-Print. When we wake up day after day and recommit to our personal beliefs and principles, we are still changing and recreating ourselves. We are also being self-disciplined. The principles we are trying to live — such as acting with integrity, being loving, being open, being courageous, being successful, being spiritual — transform and change as we grow and learn. What being loving is like at the age of 20 may be very different than at the age of 50. We are firm believers in constantly self-evaluating and practicing personal reflection. **We believe that self-evaluation is the No. 1 life skill**. Life is a process of creation, and we are re-creating ourselves day to day. Neal Donald Walsch, in his book *Conversations with God*, explains it this way: "The deepest secret is that life is not a process of discovery, but a process of creation. You are not discovering yourself, but creating yourself anew. Seek, therefore, not to find out *Who You Are*, seek to determine *Who You Want to Be*."

There are two problems facing most people: they do not apply self-discipline to creating the life they desire and most people have no clue what criteria on which to evaluate themselves. If these criteria do not exist, individuals are prone to evaluate others, worry about how others evaluate them, and evaluate what is happening *to* them. With BE-Print, the focus shifts from others to you and who you want to be in any given situation. What we hope for you is that this journey will help you construct the life of your dreams and provide you a ruler with which to measure your success. **Asking yourself daily "Who do I want to be in this situation?" is a habit that can help you each and every day in all sorts of situations.** Glenn is fond of saying, "Just as an architect needs a blueprint to build a structure, a person needs a BE-Print to build a life." That is what this book is about: you creating your own unique BE-Print to become the person you really want to be.

Parts of the BE-Print (beliefs, principles, and actions) perform together like a well-executed freestyle swim — arms, legs, breathe, and rhythm all working together in harmony. We are going to talk a lot about alignment among the components of your BE-Print. Living in alignment allows you to create a harmonious life, one in which you practice your beliefs on a regular basis. When people act in alignment to their beliefs and principles, they experience less stress, which is then reflected in all areas of their lives — mind, body, and spirit. We believe the processes of alignment and self-evaluation are missing from the lives of many people. To encourage alignment, you will be asked to look at what principles you are living that represent your beliefs, and then what actions you are taking in relation to those principles.

Along the way, we will share how we ourselves and others have put these ideas into practice. We thank each of them for their willingness to share their lives with our readers. We also believe in modeling as the No. 1 teaching strategy. *Practicing what we teach* is who we want to be as facilitators. We each have our own BE-Print and we are continually updating them. Portions of our individual BE-Prints appear on our website under "About Us." You are welcome to visit us often and see how we are engaging in our own conscious process of revision and self-evaluation. As facilitators, we try to be entertaining, practical, humorous, and in depth. We have tried to incorporate all of these qualities into this book, as well.

As you wade into the process of creating your BE-Print, please remember we want to see you swim through life with grace and style, becoming the person you have always wanted to be. We would love you to share your experiences with us and other swimmers along the way. You will find a section on our website for just that purpose. We hope you will be encouraged by your own progress and the success of others as you make this journey. No one said it better then the ancient Chinese philosopher Lao Tzu: "The journey of a thousand miles begins with one step." Or one stroke — stroke of the pen, that is.

What is one reason you picked up this book and started reading it?

7

■ *What do you hope will be different when you finish reading it?*

A Path to Creating

"As you think, so you are.
As you dream, so you
become. As you create
your wishes, so they
create you."

Wendy Garrett

You may have heard the expression *Rome wasn't built in a day*. Well, Rome wasn't built by accident either. The coliseum, the pantheon, Saint Peter's basilica, the Trevi fountain... all architectural marvels were created through forethought and exploration. They were created only after architects and artists had spent countless hours developing what we would now call blueprints of the buildings' foundations and structural frameworks and considered aesthetic appeal.

A blueprint, as the outline of the building plan, is a vitally important document. Even so, the blueprint only represents a small step in the planning process. Before a building or a work of art can be constructed, its planners must also consider what raw materials to use, what will enhance the present landscape, the functionality of the building, the message or emotion they want to convey and determine how to proceed. A good building plan starts with a blueprint, but extends far beyond it. It's hard to achieve anything consequential without forethought and a written plan. However, putting a plan on paper isn't enough. Regardless of how thorough, concrete, or ingenious a plan may be, it won't happen unless additional ingredients are injected into the planning process. Leadership expert John C. Maxwell writes about two key ingredients in planning: *passion* and *flexibility*. He states that passion gives planning energy and that flexibility allows you to see new opportunities when your plans don't go as expected. Your BE-Print is like a blueprint that serves as the foundational document for creating the life of your dreams. Like the process of creating a great work of art or architecture, creating the *you* that you have always wanted to be requires more than just a written plan. For this reason, the BE-Print system is more than just a document.

The BE-Print system is composed of three major components:

- Self-discipline.
- Self-reflective exercises captured in the BE-Print document.
- Continuous self-evaluation.

Like the support columns on a building, self-discipline and self-evaluation scaffold the framework of the BE-Print document. Together they form a sustainable, principled, centered life. Originally, the BE-Print system grew out of PCT programs we developed for our work with individuals, schools, families, businesses, and other organizations. In 2005, Shelley and Glenn created and implemented the original BE-Print as part of the Personal Life Skills courses at the Mecklenburg County Jail in Charlotte, North Carolina. When they returned to the community, every inmate who graduated from the course was equipped with a BE-Print to use in daily self-evaluation. Glenn then began using this concept with private clients and Shelley with educators. BE-Print is a detailed agreement an individual makes with himself to define and describe the person he wants to be and serves as his personal yardstick for self-evaluation. The BE-Print has now become an integral component in programs for individuals young and old, educators and students, parents and children, management and employees, correctional officers and adjudicated juveniles and adults, and coaches and their players. The value in the BE-Print system comes in the flexibility of people to recognize, define, and evaluate their lives based on what is important to them, rather than wasting their time worrying about how others evaluate them. Passion and flexibility are built into the process.

Adults often ask children, "Who do you want to be when you grow up?" What most folks mean by this is *what are you going to do to make money when you get older?* We think these adults are asking the right question, but wanting the "wrong" answer. When adults asked you this as a kid, their intent wasn't to ask you to explore your beliefs and principles and how you would live these on a daily basis. For many of you, this will be the first time anyone has asked you this question looking for the "right" answer. The intent of our question is deeper and more complex than pondering career paths.

Off the top of your head, what is one belief you have about nature?

What is one principle you try to live by each day that reflects this belief?

The second question is not so easy to answer, is it? If, however, we ask you what you "do" for a living, you can probably describe it in detail without much thought. What our experience has taught us, working with people from across the globe, is that you are not much different from most folks out there. The few we run into that know who they are trying to be in the world are less stressed, appear to be more comfortable in their lives, and in general are a whole lot healthier. Being healthier by relieving stress is one of the big reasons to create a BE-Print.

We define *stress* as a perceived inability to control. So what do we mean by control? Many people see the word *control* as cold, technical, and mechanical. We think of it in a different way. In PCT, control is what living is all about. Situations or people are often described as "out of control." At the core of this statement is the idea that being "in control" is valuable and being "out of control" isn't so great.

According to William Powers, **behavior is the control of perception**. Controlling is the process by which all living systems maintain the conditions that they want. It is the process a sunflower uses to get enough sunlight; it is the process a baby uses to get rid of a sensation of hunger; it is the process your body uses to pump blood throughout your body to maintain the delivery of oxygen and nutrients to your cells. It is also the process you use to build the life you desire, to bring about the relationships you cherish, and to create the career of your dreams. For us *behavior* and *control* are synonymous. Behavior does not consist solely of the actions we take; actions are one part of what we do to maintain control. As humans, we like to think our actions are conscious choices. However, if you accept a PCT explanation of behavior, our systems simply do what is necessary to maintain control, to maintain a specific condition. Humans are living control systems in which each individual is constantly changing her desired state.

TECHNICAL NOTE: **Control Systems**

In science and engineering, these types of systems are called "negative feedback control systems." Common examples of nonliving control systems are the cruise control in your car and the thermostat in your house. In both of these systems, you specify a desired state (speed or temperature) and the "system" takes action to adjust to the environment. The system is designed to get a match between the present and the desired speed or temperature.

This very basic process of constantly comparing *what we want* (our **reference**) to *what we are recording* (our **perception**) and taking action to get a closer match is about getting things "just right." **Control involves these three basic components: action, perception, and comparison.** Controlling is the essence of living.

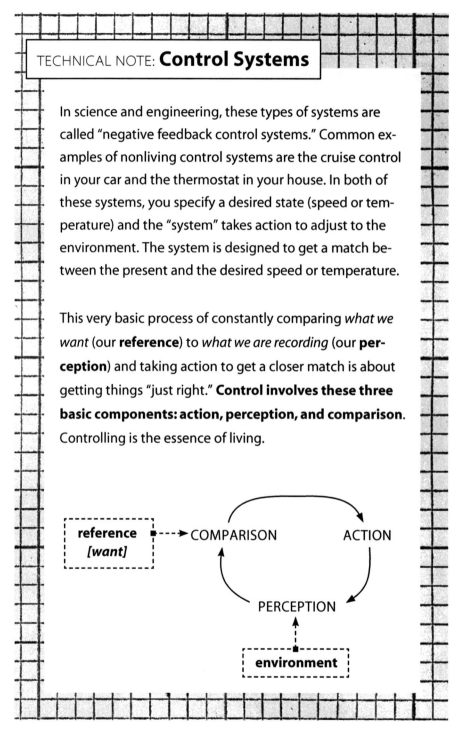

To be healthier means to be more consciously in control of our lives. To do this, we need to take three easy foundation-building steps. These steps lay the foundation of the BE-Print. The first step is to tune into what we really want in our lives and specifically in the five areas of **health**, **wealth**, **relationships**, **intellectual growth**, and **spirituality**. If we carefully define our personal "just right" in each of these areas, we will be more likely to look for opportunities to bring these into our lives. We can then compare our "just rights" to our perceptions of our present life. Doing so will help us look for areas of growth and help us feel more in control. We need to remember that we have the ability to change both what we want and how we perceive our world. Granted, it is usually easier to change what we desire, but with time and practice we can change how we perceive incoming information. Along the way we may also learn skills to more effectively and efficiently act on the environment to get more of our "just rights." Through clearly defining our wants and learning how changing our actions and perceptions guide us to achieving our "just rights" we can take more effective control of our lives.

You may be wondering why we chose to focus on these five areas. The answer is two-fold. First, health, wealth, and relationships are the three areas most reported sources of stress in people's lives. In fact, some research indicates that 95 percent of reported stress comes from these three areas. The last two areas, intellect and spirituality, address our wholeness as a human in mind, body, and spirit. We have found that if life in these five areas is "under control" you are more likely to relieve stress, be healthy, and become the person you have always wanted to be.

The second step we need to take is to look into each of these five areas and answer the question, *Which part of this can I control?* Glenn calls this the serenity prayer question. We often try to control things that are impossible for us to control. We think we can control other people or override our genetic make-up or determine who is laid off when an employer down-sizes. When we understand PCT, we emphasize personal responsibility, internal motivation, and control as maintaining a specified condition, and let go of trying to change things that are out of our control.

Serenity Prayer

God, grant me the serenity
To accept the things I cannot change;
The courage to change the things that I can;
And the wisdom to know the difference.

The third foundation-building step is to practice alignment of our beliefs, principles, and actions. We need to align our beliefs in each area of our lives with the principles we try to live by, and then we need to monitor how we spend our time and energy so that what we do is in tune with our beliefs. If I believe in abundance and I live the principle of being generous, then I will view requests for time or money donations to a cause I believe in as an opportunity, not an obligation. My use of my time, energy, and resources will be aligned with my principles and beliefs. Alignment is monitored through continuous self-evaluation.

The BE-Print system is designed to help you help yourself by becoming more self-disciplined; understand the process of control so that you can better manage your emotions; define and align your beliefs, principles, and actions; and provide you an instrument to measure your personal success and to habitually self-evaluate. A few minutes of introspection can help us journey through life with a lot less stress!

What is one area of your life in which you exhibit self-discipline?

How might letting go of worrying about how others evaluate you affect you?

Examining Your Beliefs

"Making a deep change involves abandoning both present knowledge and competence, then 'walking naked' into the land of uncertainty."

Robert Quinn

Walking the labyrinth is an ancient meditative art form designed to serve as a metaphor of one's life journey. An ancient symbol that relates to wholeness, the labyrinth meditation is intended to help the walker circle inward to the center of her soul to the deepest self and back out into the world with a broadened understanding of who she is. By returning via the same path, the walker begins to integrate the lessons learned into daily living.

Each person's walk is a personal experience, just as how one walks and what one receives differs with each passage. Some people use the walk for clearing the mind and centering. Others enter with a question or concern in order to create or envision a solution. At the center it is believed the walker can release inner emotions as one turns around in order to work one's way back.

Labyrinths are not mazes consisting of twists, turns, and blind alleys. A maze is like a puzzle to be solved. It is a left brain task that requires logical, sequential, analytical activity to find the correct path into the maze and out. A labyrinth has only one path. It is unicursal, a path that is created without lifting your pencil. The way in is the way out. There are no blind alleys. The path leads you on a circuitous path to the center and out again. A labyrinth is a right brain task. It involves intuition, creativity, and imagery. When you walk a labyrinth, you meander back and forth, turning 180 degrees each time you enter a different circuit. As you shift your direction you also shift your awareness from right brain to left brain. It is a journey into wholeness or oneness, connecting your mind, body, and spirit.

Much like walking a meditational labyrinth, the creation of the BE-Print is a journey in which each step along the path is meant to be savored and enjoyed. It is a process where the way in is the way out. Its development is intended to take you to the core of who you want to be and back again, to living that life each and every moment of every day. It is intended to help you align your beliefs, principles, and actions. The BE-Print is a document that will serve as your personal yard stick for becoming the person you want to be and a tool for self-evaluation. The process of its development will take you to the center of yourself and back out again. This journey brings meaning to life.

Like many journeys, creating and living your BE-Print requires self-discipline, taking one more step when that step may seem impossible. Being honest with yourself, digging deep, being patient and sticking with it will all be part of the journey. If you are looking for a quick-fix solution, creating and living your BE-Print isn't it. You will have to give yourself credit for those areas that are working for you and recognize those areas that aren't.

Kerry Hardy, a former student, a friend, and a colleague, talks about becoming "teachable." You must be willing to say, "Hey, I don't know this." You need to be willing to listen to that small voice inside yourself that recognizes that *not knowing* is a learning opportunity, not a crisis. In the development of your BE-Print you are your own teacher. Recognizing what you know and what you don't know about yourself is essential. The first step in any change process is awareness. Awareness of the gap between who you are today and who you want to become means being honest with yourself; you cannot change what you don't acknowledge. The most famous book on change and the oldest known classic Chinese text, the *I Ching*, helps us understand ourselves better and derive more from life. The book is based on an ever-changing life, in an ever-changing world, where understanding ourselves gives us strength to confront everyday life. This is the premise on which the BE-Print was developed.

In PCT, we call the highest level of perception the *systems lev-el*. This first circuit of your personal labyrinth encompasses your conceptual beliefs, your constructs, and your sense of self. Peter Senge in his book *The Fifth Discipline* calls these constructs *mental models*. He writes: "Mental models are deeply held internal images of how the world works, images that limit us to familiar ways of thinking and acting." Knowing how you think the world works and in particular what you believe to be your place in the world is essen-tial to getting at the core of who you want to be. An old Hispanic adage puts it this way: "Every head has a different world."

We all have conceptual beliefs that play a critical role in our lives. Many of us do not often take the time to examine them and reflect on how they are serving or not serving us. Our mental mod-els strongly influence the principles we live by and the actions we take. Taking time to reflect on your basic beliefs based on your sys-tems level concepts can help you align your life, take more effective control of your life, and relieve stress. Start by looking at the belief statements listed below and think about whether you agree with them. Then place an "X" on the continuum from strongly agree to strongly disagree that reflects your level of agreement with the stated belief.

Belief Statements

	STRONGLY AGREE				STRONGLY DISAGREE

■ All work has value and dignity.. . . . .☐ ☐ ☐ ☐ ☐

■ We all have the ability to create our lives;
it is not a matter of destiny or fate. . . . .☐ ☐ ☐ ☐ ☐

■ Things inside of us make us do the things
we do. . . . .☐ ☐ ☐ ☐ ☐

■ Things outside of us make us do the things
we do. . . . .☐ ☐ ☐ ☐ ☐

■ Adults' beliefs and values are determined
by their experiences. . . . .☐ ☐ ☐ ☐ ☐

■ Men are superior to women and children. . .☐ ☐ ☐ ☐ ☐

■ Wisdom comes with age. . . . .☐ ☐ ☐ ☐ ☐

■ There is a supreme being that holds us
accountable. . . . .☐ ☐ ☐ ☐ ☐

■ There is not enough to go around. The
world consists of the "haves" and "have nots."
It's survival of the fittest. . . . .☐ ☐ ☐ ☐ ☐

■ Some people are born with more potential
than others. . . . .☐ ☐ ☐ ☐ ☐

■ There are moral absolutes (rules of right and
wrong) that apply to all people in every culture. .☐ ☐ ☐ ☐ ☐

■ People are basically evil. . . . .☐ ☐ ☐ ☐ ☐

■ *Write two or three strong beliefs you have that are not on the list.*

Now try challenging your beliefs a bit by asking yourself to dig deeper. When you thought about whether "all work has value and dignity," did you think in terms of all legal work? Would that change your answer? How much of your life do you really believe you can control? A core concept of PCT is that neither the things inside of us nor the things outside of us make us do what we do. Rather, *it is the relationship between the two that makes us do what we do.*

> *A core concept of PCT is that neither the things inside of us nor the things outside of us make us do what we do. Rather, it is the relationship between the two that makes us do what we do.*

Do you believe that? Why or why not?

Think of the statement: *Adults' beliefs and values are determined by their experiences.* What meaning do you put on the word *determine*? Would your answer change if you thought of the word *influence* rather than *determine*? If men are superior to women and children, what constitutes superior? How are men and women alike, and how are they different? What role do you believe children play in our society and how has this changed over time? Does wisdom come with age or does it come through experience? Are we accountable to a higher power? Do you believe in God? A collective consciousness? A supreme being? Does it matter how you label it? Is this an abundant world? Is it simply a matter of reallocating resources? What's your personal potential? Does hard work play a role in success or is it more a matter of innate ability? If there are moral absolutes, is it ever OK to kill someone? What about during war? Or to protect your loved ones? Are we born "neutral" and our life experiences move us toward being good or evil? Time for some self-evaluation. Are you being absolutely honest here? Are you digging deeper? Are you reflecting on your core beliefs? Did you examine some long-held beliefs and ask yourself *do I really believe this*?

Take a few minutes to evaluate whether your long-held beliefs hold up to intense scrutiny. Jot down your thoughts.

How often have you said, "That's the way I am," or "That's the way it is"? Those specific words point to what you *believe* to be true. If we were taught as a child that the world is out to get us, then everything we hear that fits that belief we accept as the truth. Anything that doesn't fit within that framework gets ignored. On the other hand, if we were taught early in life that the world is a safe place, then we would hold other beliefs. We could easily accept that love is everywhere, and people are basically friendly, and we will always have what we need. Often, what we believe is based on someone else's opinion that we have unconsciously adopted. This is a chance to identify core beliefs that may not really be your own. Remember that you are in charge of your thoughts. Take some time to examine your thoughts and set yourself free!

Ask yourself: Where do my beliefs come from? Who were the people, places, and events that influenced me most? Do my beliefs come from trying to fit in with friends? Do they come from my grandparents? Do they come from the music I listen to, the people I hang out with, the programs I watch on TV?

Write down three or four people, places, or events that helped form your beliefs.

Beliefs are repeated thoughts. When we keep running the same thoughts, we begin to think that's the way the world is. We then either adopt or rebel against that belief. Our beliefs reflect the way we think the world is, or the way we think we are. When we think about ourselves the same way over and over again, telling the same story about who we are, pretty soon we accept that that's the way we are.

Let's take a closer look at your beliefs about yourself and about how the world works, starting with you! The words *I am* are two of the most powerful words in the English language. When you say "*I am* _____" you create who you are. At the higher levels we believe many people have a reference for living a life of purpose and meaning. However, each person defines that purpose in his own way. There is a link between how you define *purpose* and how you describe the person you *want* to be. For example, if you believe that knowledge is power (and you want power), then you want to be a person who is knowledgeable. If you believe that people should be hard working, then you want to be a hard worker. Ask yourself some very simple questions about your beliefs about who you want to be that define for you a purposeful life:

1. ***In the first column, answer this question:***
    ▓ What do I repeatedly say or think about myself?
    (I am _____.)

2. ***One at a time, look at each belief about yourself and ask:***
    ▓ How does this characteristic link to my personal definition of purpose? (Why is it important to me?)
    ▓ Where did this belief come from?
    ▓ How has this belief served me or not served me?

3. ***After you examine each statement, ask yourself...***
    ▓ Would I be better served if I threw out or revised this belief and began to tell a new story?
    ▓ What would I shift this belief to if I wanted to change it?

I am...   *My thoughts on this belief about myself...*

There are two ideas here about beliefs: (1) Who you *want* to be, which is a reflection of what you value and find meaningful. (2) Who you believe you *are* (how you define yourself right now). The first can be thought of as your reference, the second is your present *self-perception*. When there is a mismatch between who you want to be and who you believe you are, your system is in a constant state of error or stress. Shifting either the *want* or the *self-perception* can reduce stress.

We have provided some examples to get your thinking started.

I am...	SHIFT: *I am...*
I am fat.	I am healthy.
I am charismatic.	I am of substance.
I am creative.	
I am spiritual.	
I am talkative.	I am a good communicator.

Some items listed in the first column — repeated thoughts that you have about yourself — don't need to be shifted. These are beliefs that serve you well and help give your life purpose.

Some items in the first column may be shifted in the second column to better align with what you find meaningful. For example, we are both talkers. Being talkative by nature is neither good nor bad. Most of the time that quality has served us well, however sometimes we find we need to stop talking and listen. Being a good communicator, however, is an aspect of ourselves that helps give purpose to our lives by helping others understand complicated ideas, leading workshops, and developing instructional materials. A good communicator is a reference more closely aligned to who we want to be.

Notice that everything in the second column — the column that is written as a want or a desire — is written in the affirmative and is readily attainable. Instead of "I am fat" Being shifted to "I am not fat" or "I am skinny," it was shifted to "I am healthy." Being healthy is a *want* and it is much more doable than being skinny. Too often people think in terms of what they don't want (I don't want to be fat) or set targets that are out of immediate reach (I want to be skinny). Your chance of success in shifting to the new you is greater if you stretch yourself, not exhaust yourself.

Now it's your turn...

I am... SHIFT: *I am...*

For each item you wrote in the first column, answer the following questions:

- How does this characteristic link to my personal definition of purpose? (Why is it important to me?)

- Where did this belief come from?

- How has this belief served me or not served me?

- Would I be better off if I dropped or revised that belief and began to tell a new story?

- How can I shift this belief to better serve me?

Just as we have beliefs about ourselves, we have beliefs about the world and how it works. Maybe you believe that "someday God will judge me for what I did with my life." Or maybe you believe "to be a man I gotta control my woman." Or that "success is about having lots of money." We need to take a closer look at these repeated thoughts to decide if they are helping us become the person we want to be. The fastest path to long-term change is changing your thinking. Whatever the problematic belief is, it comes from a thought pattern, and *thought patterns can be changed!* Until you recognize the connection between your outer experiences and your inner thoughts and beliefs, you allow yourself to take on the role of victim. For example:

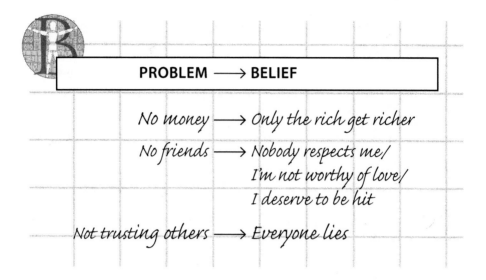

PROBLEM $\longrightarrow$	BELIEF
No money $\longrightarrow$	Only the rich get richer
No friends $\longrightarrow$	Nobody respects me/
	I'm not worthy of love/
	I deserve to be hit
Not trusting others $\longrightarrow$	Everyone lies

Remember you are the only person who can think for you! No one is in a better position to evaluate you than you. You are the power and authority in your world! Take some time to record a couple of core beliefs in each of the five areas: relationships, health, wealth, intellect, and spirituality. If these five areas don't work for you, feel free to change one or all of them. Just keep the list short for now. Be sure that *you* really accept them as truth and that they will serve you both now and in the long run to become the person you have always wanted to be.

Relationships

Health

Wealth

Intellect

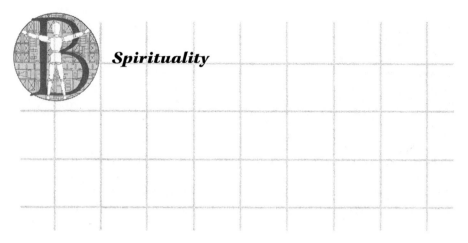

Spirituality

Remember that in the BE-Print process, self-evaluation happens all the time. This isn't a one-time deal. It is something you need to be aware of all the time, and check in on a regular basis. Just as a snake sheds its skin so it can grow, people need to self-evaluate so they can create the life they want.

If you could accept one new belief about yourself, what would it be and how would it serve you better?

How honest were you with yourself when defining your beliefs?

Establishing Principles

"We're all pilgrims on the
same journey – but some
pilgrims have better
road maps."

Nelson DeMille

At the center of everything we think, do, or say lie our beliefs, consciously or unconsciously guiding our lives. In the last chapter, we asked you to examine your beliefs in order for you to be more conscious of them. We also asked you to examine which beliefs have and have not served you well. We asked you to keep the ones that you believed were serving you well and change those that you thought were not. The first step in any change process is aware-ness and attention. **In the language of PCT, consciousness is perception plus awareness.** *Perceiving* is the process by which we record the world, both inside and outside of us. Like a massive calculator, billions of bits of information are received and recorded as a single perception. Our perceptions for the most part are unconscious. We are not talking about cognition, we are talking about the process of using the senses to acquire information about the surrounding environment or situation. It would be virtually impossible to be aware of each and every one of the billions of bits of information flooding our systems. However, when we are able to focus our attention on the higher levels of perception (like what our beliefs are and what principles guide us) we can better manage our lives.

In PCT, behavior is the control of perception. Understanding what you want and how you perceive your world is critical to becoming the person you really want to be. By drawing attention to and expanding your awareness of some of your beliefs, you are now able to take more conscious actions — actions that are more aligned to the core of who you are. Human beings have the capacity to grow and change. All aspects of our nature — physical, mental, emotional, and spiritual — can be developed and become complementary to each other when we have a vision of what is possible and are clear on who we want to be in the world. When we are consciously aware of our beliefs, we take the first step in taking more effective control of our lives. Repeated thinking about our personal principles, standards, values, and generalizations create our beliefs. It is at the principles level of perception that we will ask you next to explore and establish a core set of principles from which to operate in all facets of your life. Changing our internal dialog (thinking) can change any part of us (mind, body, or spirit).

When we go about living, our beliefs decide what principles to control for. These principles define the ethical and moral standards you use to make decisions and to take action. Principles are second only to beliefs in the hierarchy of control; they are another set of references that guide your thoughts, actions, and emotions. Why do we say that they guide your daily activities? Because at any given moment you are trying to match the reference (or want) you are aware of to the information you are processing about the world. "Be loving" is a principle that is at the heart of almost all organized religions. When someone adopts that principle as his own, he can then ask himself, *What would it look like to "be loving" in this situation?* When we live by our principles, they act as flexible guidelines for a multitude of situations. They are not rules to follow or strategies that apply in a limited number of situations or to specific problems. All living things operate based on principles, regardless of whether they are aware of them or obedient to them. Take a plant, for example. One of the principles it follows to stay alive is to grow its roots towards the water. You may have heard the saying a dog never bites the hand that feeds it. That is a principle that most domesticated animals live by. The qualities that define us are a direct reflection of both our principles and beliefs.

Living based on a set of principles allows us to step back and look at ourselves from a distance. Stephen Covey, in his work on becoming principle-centered, states: "As a principle-centered person, you try to stand apart from the emotion of the situation and from other factors that would act upon you, and evaluate the options."

When you are able to do this, you are more in control of your life and experience less stress.

Christians believe the beatitudes expressed in Matthew 5: 3-12 were Christ's message intended to guide, teach, and show what values to live by. Matthew writes, "Blessed are the poor in spirit, the meek, those that hunger and thirst for righteousness, those that are merciful, those that are pure in heart, the peacemakers, and those that are persecuted for righteousness sake." Living these principles guide Christians on a path to experiencing a state of peace and happiness. What "BE-attitudes" or principles do you want to guide your life? If you are like most people, you probably haven't stopped to think much about it, and when you do you aren't sure where to begin.

Over the past five years, we have asked hundreds of individuals this same question. *What principles do you want to live your life by?* Most often, this question is answered with silence and a perplexed look. We have learned to jump-start people's thinking by providing them with a list of possibilities. Feel free to add or subtract from the list. There is no magic in the number of principles we listed, the wording we chose, or the definitions provided. The list is constantly under revision. What you have here has come from our experience in working with people of all ages and cultures. If you do add some principles of your own just remember that **the key is BE!** Each word that is added should be a principle that can guide you in life.

First read through the entire list of principles we've outlined. Think about how you habitually act, think, and speak and how these behaviors align with your values and beliefs. Ask yourself how you *want to be*. If one of your life principles doesn't appear on the list, add it. Identify it as a way of *being*, and then define it. Then rank order your principles from 1 to 18 with No. 1 being the most important to you at this time and 15 through 18 being less important right now. Test the waters. Dive on in. We will be here when you surface.

Principles

BE JUST

RANKING

Being impartial or fair; conforming to truth, fact, or reason; treating everyone equally.

BE GRATEFUL

RANKING

Recognizing what you have instead of focusing on what you don't. Appreciating the beauty and miracle of life.

BE LOYAL

RANKING

Being a friend; being intimate. Remaining faithful and/or devoted to a person, group or cause.

BE COMPETENT *Being skilled. Recognizing your ability to do something well. Being successful, knowledgeable, proficient, and capable.*

RANKING

BE WISE *Combining experience and knowledge with the ability to apply them strategically. Using common sense and being discerning. Knowing the intelligent thing to do.*

RANKING

BE HONORABLE *Possessing integrity and steadfastly adhering to high moral principles and professional standards. Being honest, sincere, and truthful.*

RANKING

BE TOLERANT *Accepting and honoring the differing views and beliefs of others. Being fair to those who hold differing views.*

RANKING

BE INDEPENDENT

RANKING

Being self-determining without outside hindrance or restraint. Being self-regulating. Standing on your own; being responsible and accountable.

BE LOVING

RANKING

Having affection based on admiration and concern for the welfare of self and others; being respectful, compassionate, caring, kind, and benevolent.

BE CREATIVE

RANKING

Being able to make imaginative use of limited resources, to think outside the box, and to be artistic, visionary, and ingenious.

BE HEALTHY

RANKING

Being sound in mind, body, and spirit and freed from physical disease or pain; having a sense of well being.

BE SPIRITUAL

RANKING

Showing great refinement and concern for the more ethereal things in life; being non-materialistic. Recognizing a relationship with a religious or non-religious higher power.

BE COURAGEOUS

RANKING

Acting despite fear or lack of confidence. Having bravery, guts, and valor.

BE PLAYFUL

RANKING

Being fond of having fun; being good-humored and lighthearted. Laughing and enjoying the moment.

BE SELF-DISCIPLINED

RANKING

Habitually exercising self-control, moderation, balance, and will power.

BE   *Definition:*

_____

RANKING

BE   *Definition:*

_____

RANKING

BE   *Definition:*

_____

RANKING

Welcome back! So how was it? What we have found is that some people struggle with the forced choice aspect of this activity. In other cases, we have found that people liked to make a choice from a list, and that they had struggled with the open-endedness of the beliefs exercise in the last chapter. You will notice we keep using the word *exercise*. Exercise is a task or activity that is performed regularly as a way of practicing and improving a skill or procedure.

The intent of exercise is to keep a person fit and healthy. The term is used here to remind you to keep coming back and exercising your self-evaluation muscles. Focusing on all eighteen principles can be overwhelming, so we suggest you focus on your top five.

Take a few minutes to reflect upon your thought process as you rank ordered your principles. Think about what in your experience has led you to want to be this type of a person. Was it something you learned from mistakes you made? Was it something you saw someone else do repeatedly? Was it something that you believe successful people do? Where did your thinking come from? Jot down a couple of ideas.

My thoughts...

Principles are at the second highest level of perception. Perceptions at this level are generalizations, criteria, and standards. Different combinations of perceptions at this level combine to form our beliefs. **There should be a link between your beliefs and your principles.** For many people, this is unexplored territory. According to Stephen Covey in *7 Habits of Highly Effective People*, "Principles are deep fundamental truths that have universal application. They apply to individuals, to marriages, to families, to private and public organization of every kind." As introduced in the beginning of this book, when you were younger, people often asked you who you wanted to be when you grew up. What they were really asking was what you wanted to do with your life. Did you want to become a firefighter, a teacher, a preacher, an engineer, a graphic designer? Although the question was framed as a "be" question, it reflected a lower level of perception. In PCT, we call this lower level the program level. (We will further explore the levels of perception later in the book.) What we are asking you to think about now is a much deeper farther-reaching question: **Who do you really want to be in the world?** What key principles do you want to permeate your life? Covey says, "When these truths are internalized into habits, they empower people to create a wide variety of practices to deal with different situations." Think about one of your principles that has been a habit for you for a very long time, perhaps even from the time you were a young child. In the area provided, list as many different situations as possible and people with whom you were able to live this principle. (It doesn't have to be one of your top five principles.)

Principle: _____

◼ *How I live this principle...*

Now think about a principle that may be a recent addition to your top-five list. Perhaps as a child, you were not very focused on your sense of spirituality or you didn't really care about being tolerant. Why do you believe it is important to you now, when it wasn't when you were younger? Perhaps you had no role models to show you how to live this principle. Maybe you are in a different role now, as a parent or grandparent, and therefore your priorities have changed. Are there other principles that have changed over time? How might your ranking change ten years from now? Record a few thoughts about the changing prioritization of your principles.

Changing principles and priorities...

Establishing your top five principles is meaningless unless you figure out how to integrate them into your daily life. Misalignment of a person's principles to one's beliefs and an inability to live by those principles contribute to stress. We are going to spend some time on really exploring living your principles. We will start by looking at ways you have been living your principles and examining how your principles can act as a guide in your life.

Throughout the day, you take actions — thinking, saying, and doing all sort of things, interacting with other, and traveling from place to place. Each of these actions can be an opportunity to exhibit the principles you have established. Take your No. 1 principle and write a list of people, places, activities, thinking, and self-talk that are opportunities for you to live your principle. Each of us has provided an example of one of our top five principles from our own BE-Prints to help you get started.

Glenn's Principle: **BE HEALTHY**

■ *People: family, Steven, running mates*

■ *Places: YMCA, mountains, local trails*

■ *Activities: Running, walking, stretching in the morning, drinking water, eating fruit & nuts, being still, hiking with my son, playing basketball with my daughter*

Thinking: *Attitude of gratitude, saying thank you when getting out of bed in the morning*

Self-talk: *"Woo… I'm good looking!"*
"My wife is one lucky woman."

***Shelley's Principle:* BE SPIRITUAL**

People: *Book club, Twyla, Kelli, drumming group, inmates, children (my own and others)*

Places: *The lake, church, concerts, the beach, nature*

Activities: *Meditation, drumming, listening to music, listening to uplifting books on CD, reading*

Thinking: *If you look for the good in people that's what you will find. Everyone is a bundle of potential waiting to be ignited. All of nature is precious and worth our respect. Children are our greatest asset; we need to cherish and nurture them.*

Self-talk: *"What lessons are you teaching by what you are doing?" "I am worthy of love." "I intend, desire, and graciously accept that I am working for my greater good and the greater good of others."*

Examine each of your top five principles in the same way. Notice how often you repeat the same people, places, activities, thinking, and self-talk. You may find that some things appear in all five. You may begin to recognize you are practicing some principles more than others.

1st Principle _____

People:

Places:

Activities:

Thinking:

Self-talk:

2nd Principle _____

■ *People:*

■ *Places:*

■ *Activities:*

■ *Thinking:*

■ *Self-talk:*

3rd Principle _____

■ *People:*

■ *Places:*

■ *Activities:*

■ *Thinking:*

■ *Self-talk:*

4th Principle _____

■ *People:*

■ *Places:*

■ *Activities:*

■ *Thinking:*

■ *Self-talk:*

5th Principle _____

People:

Places:

Activities:

Thinking:

Self-talk:

Think about how you practice these principles with yourself. For example, if you want to be loving and you engage regularly in negative self-talk, are you living your principles? You are the one person you will be in a relationship with for your entire life. If you are not practicing your principles with yourself as well as others, are you really living them? Practicing your principles with yourself is a healthy thing to do. You may have noticed that we are not talking about receiving, we are talking about being. When we think we want to be loved and we are not being loving, we are creating stress in our lives. The stress comes from trying to control something we cannot. A big part of living your BE-Print is recognizing what you can control and what you cannot control. People can control who they want to be; they cannot control what they receive from others.

Place your five principles in front of you. Take a few minutes to analyze what you have written. Look for trends, gaps, and opportunities. What do you notice?

As you reflect on your principles, what have you learned about yourself?

Does anything surprise you about what you've written?

What was the easiest principle to write about and what area was most difficult?

The same principles that govern our personal quality performance also lead to increased professional and organizational effectiveness. How might you live your principles in your professional life? What would be different if your entire organization aligned its practices to its beliefs and principles?

Consciously living your principles can help guide your decisions and handle difficult situations. Look at your top five principles and reflect on how they might speak to you in the following situations.

Reflect on how you might live by your principles in these scenarios. Jot down your thoughts.

When there is little or no money in your pocket.

When you don't want to get out of bed in the morning.

When someone you care about doesn't act the way you want him or her to.

Is there a difficult situation you are trying to work through right now? How might your principles influence your actions? **Establishing your principles moves you to answer the deeper question *who do I want to be* rather than the shallower question *what do I want to do.***

One of the unique things about a BE-Print is that it helps you align your life so that you can live in harmony. Look back at your principles list and the list of your beliefs in regards to relationships, health, wealth, intellect, and spirituality. Think about living your beliefs based on the top five principles you have identified. What is the relationship between your principles and beliefs? How well do they match? Do you need to do some revision to achieve better alignment? What aligns well? What needs work?

PRINCIPLE ⟶ RELATIONSHIP TO BELIEF

1.

2.

PRINCIPLE ⟶ RELATIONSHIP TO BELIEF

3.

4.

5.

When you finish, ask yourself if you need to adjust either your beliefs or principles. The BE-Print is intended to be a fluid document, so moving back and forth between the parts and reflecting on the connections and relationships is important.

We want you to tackle one last task before moving forward. We want you to reflect on how your life will be different when you are living in alignment to your principles and beliefs. Write a note to yourself, one that you plan to put away in a time capsule and open ten years from now. In the note, remind yourself about the five principles at the top of your list today. Write about them as if they have now become a part of your daily life. For example, "I am now a person who is healthy in mind, body, and spirit every day of my life. I exercise, eat healthy, and meditate every day." The more detail you provide, the greater chance you have of creating the new you that you describe.

Dear _____ ,

I am thrilled that the principles I want to live by have now become part of my character. I am now a person who. . .

When our principles become habits, we live our lives with more purpose and less stress. Stephen Covey writes about this topic in terms of developing Character Ethics, which he describes as foundational and catalytic: "The Character Ethic [teaches] that there are basic principles of effective living, and that people can only experience true success and enduring happiness as they learn and integrate these principles into their basic character." In the next part of your BE-Print, we will start moving towards integrating these principles into your life by developing your procedures, habits, rituals, and routines.

The key to becoming the person you really want to be is:

- **Becoming self-disciplined;**

- **Aligning your beliefs, principles, and actions;**

- **And continuously self-evaluating.**

Measuring your success based on what you can control and not taking someone else's temperature to see how you feel allows you to take more effective control of your life. If you want to be a happy person, you will need to start evaluating yourself more and others less.

Congratulations, you have now completed a rough draft of two parts of your BE-Print! You are on the path to becoming the person you really want to be. Take a moment and give yourself credit.

What did you learn about yourself from establishing the principles by which you want to live?

Did you think any of the information was surprising?

What shifts in your thinking and acting might you now be willing to make?

Forming Agreements

"Everything we do is based on agreements we have made – agreements with ourselves, with other people, with God, with life. But the most important agreements are the ones we make with ourselves. In these agreements we tell ourselves who we are, how to behave, what is possible, what is impossible. One single agreement is not such a problem, but we have many agreements that come from fear, deplete our energy, and diminish our self-worth."

Don Miguel Ruiz

On November 19, 1863, Abraham Lincoln gave one of the most famous speeches in American history, the Gettysburg Address. The speech was a mere 278 words in length and changed, or some would say maintained, the course set out by the founding fathers. The opening words of the speech — *"Four score and seven years ago our fathers brought forth on this continent, a new nation, conceived in Liberty, and dedicated to the proposition that all men are created equal."* — captured the beliefs and principles on which this country was founded, as defined in the Constitution of the United States. They were a reminder of the agreement the country had made with itself about who the nation wanted to be. Lincoln ended his speech with these words: *"... and that government of the people, by the people, for the people, shall not perish from the earth."* Lincoln understood and captured in the Gettysburg Address two key ideas: the first being that individuals and nations are best when grounded and guided by a set of strong beliefs and principles and the second being that constitutions are agreements of the people, by the people and for the people involved. Lincoln understood how guiding principles and agreements are especially useful in times of turmoil.

Have you ever thought about what agreements you have made with yourself and with others? What is the definition of *constitution*? Are agreements and constitutions different? Because the U.S. Constitution is so much a part of the fabric of this country, few people really take time to explore the thinking behind it. The term *constitution* refers to an agreement based on principles. The term also refers to an individual's general physical and mental health. The merging of these two definitions for *constitution* helps us understand the idea that when people make agreements based on the higher levels of perception (beliefs and principles) as to who they want to be and how they want to live, they gain a shared sense of well being. In other words, by creating a formal constitution, people can strengthen their personal constitutions. Our forefathers knew that the well-being of the nation depended on such agreements. Principles encompassed by our nation's constitution were principles such as justice, equality, liberty, and tranquility. They are captured in the opening lines: "*We the People of the United States, in Order to form a more perfect Union, establish Justice, insure domestic Tranquility, provide for the common defense, promote the general Welfare, and secure the Blessings of Liberty to ourselves and our Posterity, do ordain and establish this Constitution for the United States of America.*" These principles, along with the beliefs of the founding fathers, still guide our government today. The word *agreement* implies a consensus. In this book, we use the words *agreement* and *constitution* interchangeably. We believe both are a contract, a consensus of opinion, a promise, and a commitment to live by.

The BE-Print consists of three main agreements, the most important being the agreement you make with yourself. The other two are small group and community agreements. We can also create constitutions or agreements when working with others, such as with team members, work groups or within our larger communities. For example, Glenn's family has a constitution that defines the principles that his family has agreed to live by — individually, with each other, and in their community. Being loving, being kind, being respectful, and being productive are examples of the principles his family has incorporated into the family agreement. As a youth basketball coach, Glenn has helped several of the teams he has worked with determine what principles they wanted to uphold. In the past, his teams have agreed to be positive, be supportive, be fair, and be their best. In the courses we teach together, one of the first activities we engage in is the development of a class agreement or constitution. Many of the groups we have worked with have adopted mottos to help them remember and live both their principles and the beliefs on which they are based. Here are a few examples of team or group mottos: Win with dignity, lose with dignity. We encourage, not discourage. We learn from our mistakes. Some individual mottos are: Be for-giving, not for-getting. Be me, be free. Gandhi's expression also makes a good motto: Be the change you want to see in the world.

Like much of the BE-Print journey, a critical element to creating constitutions is the process. The process works best when a person really knows and understands herself, when she has defined her beliefs and principles. Just as the "people" created the U.S. Constitution, the participants in a group develop effective agreements where relationships have already been established. If people feel disconnected, creating an agreement is a pointless exercise. We have participated in many seminars, meetings, and discussions where the group was handed a set of "group norms" at the beginning of the session. Either we were asked to agree or it was assumed we agreed. One of the most creative was one developed by a dance instructor who put motions to each norm. They were easy to remember, but commitment was low. In almost all cases these norms worked well until strong beliefs were challenged or until something that wasn't covered on the list arose. *How agreements are formed with others is very important.* When teams, families, and classroom communities develop their own unique set of principles representing the people they want to be, these connected or shared references help groups function more effectively and serve as a standard to evaluate performance. Remember that references define the "just right," the desire, the goal, or the target. Connected references are those that a group has agreed define what members collectively want. In the hundred plus classes we have taught in the jail, no two classes have had the exact same classroom constitutions. However, two items have been agreed upon by every class: be open and be respectful.

In groups and as individuals we want to focus on people self-evaluating who they are being and how they are acting. We want the spotlight on the inside. Many individuals are more aware of what is happening outside them than what is happening internally. In other words, people tend to focus on what is happening to them, rather than who they are being in relation to these happenings. When the focus is external, thinking may go something like this: I did it because of something someone else said or something someone did. This common worldview has kept individuals and nations from taking control of their own journeys. It is time to shift that perception and to focus inward. Doing so helps us clarify what we really want for ourselves and others.

PCT emphasizes the importance of being clear on what we want. You have already taken vital first steps in doing this by examining your beliefs and establishing the principles you want to live by.

Knowing that you want to be a person who is generous helps you act in ways that are aligned with who you want to be and reduces stress. One benefit of creating a personal agreement is that one's beliefs and principles come into better focus. Personal references (what you want) also become clearer. Another benefit is that developing a personal agreement helps you live your BE-Print particularly in regards to your principles. You might think of your personal agreement as a statement of your passion put into action, your mission, what you believe is your calling. It often describes what you are compelled to do, what you can't help but do. For Shelley this has always involved teaching and for Glenn it has always been about strengthening community. How do we know this? Because when Shelley is out and about she will start teaching people almost anything, from how to bag groceries to how to hang a piece of material to serve as a drape. Glenn will constantly try to facilitate conversations, organize groups for projects, and work to get the most out of his teams. Think about how you put your passions into action.

How do you put your passions into action?

From the time I was a young child _____ _____ called to me.

I felt I was born to...

I can't help myself from doing....

I am willing to push everything else aside to ...

Now look back over your prioritized list of principles.

The five key principles I want to live are...

Before you move on, think about revisions you'd like to make to your BE-Print. Remember this is a fluid document and a fluid process — rethinking is part of the process!

What you are looking for here is reoccurring themes or a pattern over time. What strikes you as some of the key words or phrases that capture you heart, mind, body, and soul?

Record the words and phrases that touch you deep inside.

A community program that we have provided over the years is our -D-A-S-H- Juvenile Court Diversion Program. -D-A-S-H- (Developing Adolescence Strengthening Habits) is a set of courses designed to provide an educational experience to first time offenders between the ages of 12 and 16 and their families. In a nonjudgmental environment, the teens and their families learn to self-evaluate how their actions affect themselves, their families, and their communities. A cornerstone of the program is developing a Family BE-Print, which in its entirety is an agreement defining the family they really want to be. Dashes are included in the program's name to get participants to think about how they want to live their lives during their lifespan. (Think of a typical inscription on a headstone: *Born 19?? – Died 20??.*) Teens and family members are asked to think about how they want to be remembered after their *dash* on earth.

How do I want to be remembered when I no longer walk this earth? (You might want to write a personal eulogy.)

What priorities have I set for my life? What do I want to accomplish?

How does what I've thought about and written reflect my principles?

Before you pull it together into a statement here are a few hints:

- Make it emotional. Including emotional words and phrases infuses your statement with passion, inspiration, and energy.

- Keep it simple, clear, and brief. The most powerful statements tend to be three to five sentences long. They are easier to remember and keep to the point.

- Describe who you want to be, not who you don't want to be. Find the positive alternatives to any negative statements.

■ Keep reworking it. Your personal statement will continue to change and evolve as you gain insights about you, what you believe, and who you want to be.

Shelley has written hers in the form of a personal mission (agreement) statement: *"My mission is to model compassion and caring towards all living and non-living things. To help others recognize the gifts they have to offer and encourage them to give these gifts to the world. To be a passionate teacher who helps individuals take their next step in learning."*

In Glenn's BE-Print he writes: *"I want to be a man who is and will be remembered as compassionate, wise, and spiritual. I want to be the principles I believe in – they are to be loving, healthy, playful, spiritual, and of integrity. In everything I do I want to be remembered as someone who made a positive difference in the world."*

Now it's your turn to write a personal agreement.

My personal agreement...

To help you better integrate your personal mission statement into your life, try to create a couple of mottos that will remind you of your BE-Print. Mottos are short sayings that express a rule to live by. Adages, slogans, short quotes, and axioms all serve this purpose. Mottos serve as gentle reminders to reflect on who you want to be in the world. For some folks, mottos become affirmations to focus the day. Louise Hay in her book *You Can Heal Your Life* reminds us: "To look yourself straight in the eye and make a positive declaration about yourself is, in my opinion, the quickest way to get results with affirmations." Throughout her book she list hundreds of affirmations. One of our favorites is "I allow my thoughts to be free. The past is over. I am at peace."

Mottos I want to live...

If you are stuck, here are a few mottos we have heard over the years to help you unlock your mental block:

■ Be nice! My religion is kindness.

■ If you can't say something nice, say nothing at all.

■ You catch a lot more bees with honey than you do with vinegar.

■ If it is to be, it's up to me.

It might help to think of one motto for each of the five areas: relationships, health, wealth, spirituality, and intellect. Or you might think of the major roles you play in life — father, mother, sister, brother, boss, or employee — and create one motto for each. One of Glenn's mottos as a father is *Be a teacher, not a preacher.*

What brings power to agreements is accountability. Accountability is a system put into place to support one another when we struggle to maintain the agreements that we make with others and ourselves. Vital to living every agreement is asking a very important follow-up question: *"Who do I want to be when I am not being who I agreed I would be?"* What is my job as your teacher, coach, parent, counselor, manager, facilitator, or leader when you are not being the class, team, children, clients, employees, or learners that you agreed to be? Furthermore, what is your job when I am not being who I told you I would be? And who do I want to be with myself when I am not who I agreed with myself to be?

The idea here is to decide before anything happens how we will handle difficult situations. In *Creating a Life Worth Living* by Carol Lloyd, she interviews David Lloyd, a famous American painter, and asks him to talk about failure: "I would say that a quarter of work I make is a complete failure, and a quarter is a semifailure, is just okay. And maybe another quarter is good, and a quarter is really good. You have to understand that failure is built in. ... There's no artist on earth that produces everything perfectly, because that's inhuman; human beings don't work like machines, they don't pump out perfection all the time." Although, you are the one developing your agreement and you will play a role in formulating family, group, and community constitutions, you will fall short again and again. We encourage you to set standards that challenge you to stretch beyond your present practices, knowing full well that you may fall short.

Try adopting this attitude: "Set a goal and fall short, set it again and fall short, set it again, fall short again. We will still be further along than if we had not set a goal at all." This attitude helps us recognize that growth comes from challenging ourselves. Put simply, **it is OK to make a mistake**. Living this belief will mean that instead of rewarding successes or punishing mistakes, you will find a way to hold yourself accountable. And when you do fall short, you will learn ways to restore your constitution. When it comes to restoring yourself, getting back to being the person you want to be, you can think of this as *RE-Printing the BE-Print*. (The next book in the BE-Print series covers this concept in depth.)

Write a formal agreement declaring who you want to be in your family and as a member of the community. Just as the United States declared its independence from England, we believe formal declarations play a key role in living your BE-Print. After we have written any agreement — be it our personal, class, group, company, or community agreement — we ask everyone involved to sign a covenant, a solemn agreement binding to all parties. We always remind everyone involved that we do not want people to sign until they are truly committed to upholding the agreement. Once you have completed your personal agreement, we encourage you to sign the following covenant.

Personal Covenant

I_____ hereby have made an agreement with myself to be the person I want to be. I commit that I will self-evaluate on a consistent basis and, if necessary, ask friends and family members who I trust to give me honest feedback. I also understand that I will make mistakes. Instead of using punishment or guilt or excuses for any mistake, I will RE-Print my BE-Print, learn from my mistakes, and use the opportunity to shift towards being who I want to be.

We would also suggest that you form agreements in your family, in your teams, in your work groups, and in any other groups you belong to. A complete BE-Print includes an agreement with self, with family (however you define that), and with your community.

How might forming agreements help you in a difficult situation?

What unwritten agreements do you have that you now want to formalize?

Developing Procedures, Routines, Rituals, & Habits

"We are what we repeatedly do. Excellence, then, is not an act, but a habit."

■
■
■
■
■
■ Aristotle

*U*p to this point, we have asked you to circle deep inside of you and begin wading into the waters of the BE-Print journey. We have taken you through processes to explore and clarify your references at the two highest levels of perception — systems and principles. The third highest level in PCT is the *program level*. Think of references at the program level like a software program you might install on your computer, consisting of a list of instruction that tell the computer "how to perform." Perceptions at the program level are those that begin the "doing" processes within you. Actual acting on the environment, what I see of you and you see of me, doesn't happen until the very lowest level of perception, at the sensory level. All programs are littered with *what if* and *if then* thinking, what mathematicians call "bifurcation points." You may think of these as decision-making points similar to coming to a T in the road while driving and being forced to decide to go one direction or another. It is important here to remember that most of what we do is unconscious. We come to these junctures countless times a day without realizing it and we keep moving forward.

As you examined your core beliefs and principles in previous chapters, the basic question was "why." The big questions you will answer in this chapter are of the "how to" variety. Specifically, you'll explore how to live your core principles on a regular basis, until they become habits. Many self-help books at this point would ask you to create a list of steps or give you a list of how-to's. The problem is that this approach doesn't allow for the flexibility necessary in an ever-changing environment. Have you ever created a step-by-step list, tried to carry it out, and found that you ran into one problem after another? Take a simple task, like backing out of your driveway in the morning. You get in the car, reach up to open the garage door, and yikes the frost from the night before has fogged the electric eye and the door won't open. Next, you put the keys in the ignition. Oops, the key won't go in smoothly, so you have to wiggle and jiggle it a little. Didn't plan on that, did you? So finally, you are backing down the driveway, and one of the kids left a bike lying in your path. Well, you get the idea. Much of life is like this. When we create detailed plans we run the risk of constantly being riddled with errors, mismatches between what we want and what we think we are getting. In PCT terminology, *error* is the gap between what you want and what you think you are getting. Your actions are your best attempts to get that "just right" sensation, an exact match between your reference and your perception. If instead of operating on rigid plans we operate at the program level, where we can apply *what if* and *if then* thinking, we run less error and create less stress within. It's like walking around with plan B, C, D, and E already in place.

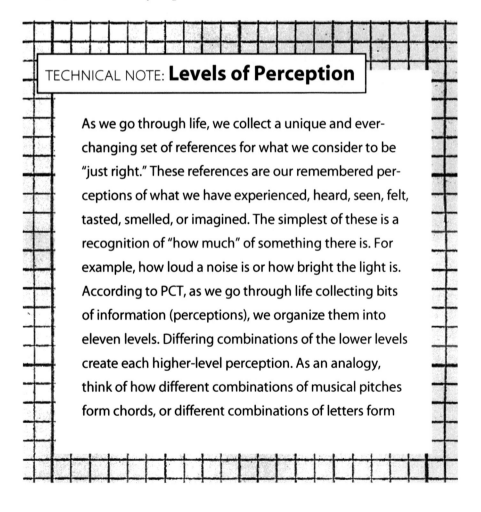

TECHNICAL NOTE: **Levels of Perception**

As we go through life, we collect a unique and ever-changing set of references for what we consider to be "just right." These references are our remembered perceptions of what we have experienced, heard, seen, felt, tasted, smelled, or imagined. The simplest of these is a recognition of "how much" of something there is. For example, how loud a noise is or how bright the light is. According to PCT, as we go through life collecting bits of information (perceptions), we organize them into eleven levels. Differing combinations of the lower levels create each higher-level perception. As an analogy, think of how different combinations of musical pitches form chords, or different combinations of letters form different words. Just as in music and writing, the more complex concepts are formed through use of simpler concepts. Notes becomes melodies, melodies become songs. Letters become words, words become sentences, and so on. For ease of understanding, you can think about the six lowest levels as *sensory*. The sensory levels of perception are the way we take the world in. The next level is *category*; perceptions at this level are the labels we give what we have taken in. The next level up is *sequence*, steps we take in a specific order. At the top of the hierarchy are the *programs*, *principles*, and *systems* level. In developing your BE-Print™ you have started at the uppermost systems level where your beliefs and conceptual understandings lie. This was intentional because, in general, we operate from the highest level of our awareness downward. The question "why" focuses our awareness upward and the question "how" focuses us downward. How you live your beliefs is a journey down the levels; why you do what you do is a journey up the levels. When we shift a belief, we shift the entire system of levels.

In our seminars we are often asked questions like "What do I do when....?" or "How would you handle...?" These are sequence level questions. The answers must be performed in a specific order.

People often ask us what to do step-by-step to manage others without using coercion. The short answer is to operate based on a few key principles and programs, rather than step-by-step sequences. When operating based on a PCT worldview and acting as a manager who encourages self-evaluation, it makes more sense to *ask, rather than tell*. The idea of asking is based on the principle *be curious* (as embodied in the motto *pull, don't push*), which in turn is based on the core idea that the answers (references) reside within the individual seeking help. Put simply, human beings are creatures that don't like being pushed. No one likes to be told what to do or who they should be. When we pull from within, we honor that the other person has the wisdom within herself to find the answer. Asking is one way to do that, and there are billions of ways to ask. It is important that the question is open-ended rather than leading. "You didn't mean to

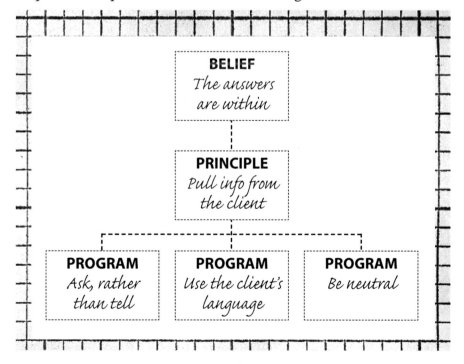

do that, did you?" or "What do you mean you're not going with me to the meeting?" are *push* questions. Asking isn't the only way to pull — body language, skilled listening, and accurately summarizing what someone else says are all ways to *pull, not push*. The next step to put your BE-Print into action is to develop a set of programs, which can be thought of as flexible rituals and routines that eventually become habits reflecting your principles.

If our beliefs and principles are in alignment, then our programs, rituals, and routines allow us to be able to adjust our actions to the nuances of the environment. The idea here is to *act out* your own core convictions. Think of how a computer program can handle many different ways of approaching the same task and yet create the same final product. Anyone that has used a personal computer for any length of time understands this. When Shelley first started using computers, she used a Mac and became familiar with each new version of its word processing program. Then Shelley switched to a PC and had to learn how to use a new program to create the same type of documents she had created before. Years later, Microsoft Office 2007 came out, and once again, she had to figure out how to do things using this new program. With each progression, the program became more and more sophisticated, yet she was still able to produce a document that looked the same as the first. Through experience, our personal programs become more and more sophisticated as well. Programs are like mazes. The most elaborate mazes have multiple paths to exit. The advantage of operating at the program level is flexibility. When Glenn would coach basketball, he applied the same principle to offenses he would create for his team. The final product would be to score a basket and stop the other team from doing so. To do that, he would develop countless offenses and defensive schemes to accomplish the same goal. He learned quickly that not only did he need numerous procedures but he also needed to encourage his players to improvise when necessary. Improvisation is often operating on key principles without running specific programs.

Flexibility at the higher levels of perception is one reason keeping our focus on these levels creates less stress within. Mark Sanborn, author of *The Fred Factor* and *The Encore Effect*, attributes one's ability to act out core convictions as one of the characteristic of successful people. In *The Encore Effect*, Sanborn asks a powerful question: "If I asked three people in your life... to use one word to describe your performance in life, what word would they choose?" The link between deep-rooted convictions and actions echoes the link we are making between living our beliefs and principles in the form of procedures, rituals, and routines. Others can clearly see who we are trying to be through our actions.

When someone first tries to change his practices, focused attention brings the gift of mindfulness. Mindfulness is bringing your awareness and focus to everything you do. Thich Nhat Hanh, a Buddhist monk, centers his teaching around conscious breathing and the awareness of each breath coupled with mindfulness of each act of daily life. He encourages people to meditate in every single act, from washing the dishes to sitting at a red light. Hanh reminds us that as humans we are often good at preparing to live but not very good at actually living.

Now that you have started to align your inner blueprint, it is time to work on conscious awareness or mindfulness of the present moment. Too often individuals fret about the past or worry about the future when the only moment available to us is now. To begin, examine what programs, rituals, and routines are so much a part of your daily life that you no longer focus your attention upon them. For example, when you first get out of bed, what do you do? When you wash dishes, clean up your living space, prepare for a meal, get ready for work, eat, or approach a new task, are there some guidelines you follow? Capture some of your thinking.

What programs, rituals, and routines could you be more mindful of?

For one week, practice being mindful while performing one of these day-to-day tasks. For example, Shelley often eats honey on an English muffin in the morning. For one week, each time she sat down to eat she would visualize the bees and flowers, hear the buzzing in the hive, smell the sweet stickiness of the honey and the perfume of the flowers, and feel the breeze and warmth of the sun on her face. Doing so allowed her to totally be in the moment, focused completely on what she was eating. At the same time, she was consciously aware of her breathing. Being mindful in simple tasks not only focuses our attention to the present moment, but also helps us clear out the chatter in our brains. This constant chatter is what often hinders your ability to live your beliefs and principles. When Glenn became aware of his morning routine through this process, he learned that his first thought in the morning was "Damn, I'm tired." Through that awareness he started consciously shifting his morning routine and began to say "Thank You" as each foot touched the floor. Awareness of your present programs is the first step to creating new rituals and routines.

During one of our recent seminars we had planned to share this idea of being mindful in simple tasks. We happened to have Thich Nhat Hanh's book *Peace Is Every Step* with us. Luckily for us, one of the participants owned a cookie shop and she brought in fresh cookies for everyone. As we prepared to eat our cookies, we read this excerpt from the book:

"When I was four years old, my mother used to bring me a cookie every time she came home from the market. I always went to the

front yard and took my time eating it, sometimes half an hour or forty-five minutes for one cookie. I would take a small bit and look up at the sky. Then I would touch the dog with my feet and take another small bite. I just enjoyed being there, with the sky, the earth, the bamboo thickets, the cat, the dog, the flowers. I was able to do that because I did not have much to worry about. I did not think of the future, I did not regret the past. I was entirely in the present moment, with my cookie, the dog, the bamboo thickets, the cat, and everything.

It is possible to eat our meals as slowly and joyfully as I at the cookie of my childhood. Maybe you have the impression that you have lost the cookie of your childhood, but I am sure it is still there, somewhere in your head. Everything is still there, and if you really want it you can find it. Eating mindfully is a most important practice of meditation. We can eat in a way that we restore the cookie of our childhood. The present moment is filled with joy and happiness. If you are attentive, you will see it."

Several participants commented afterward that this was the best cookie they had ever eaten. Still today, we both notice that if we slow down, breath, and focus while eating, the food becomes richer in flavor and our experience is more fulfilling. Being mindful brings peace to each moment.

We have learned that *a big part of creating new procedures, routines, and habits is living in the moment.* Too often we set long-term goals that are easily forgotten in our daily acts of living. When Glenn first started teaching life skills courses at the jail, he would have people set goals. For years, Shelley would facilitate goal-setting sessions with schools. As their understanding of PCT grew, they both began to realize that people have goals at all levels. Beliefs are goals, principles are goals, programs are goals, and so on down the levels of perception all the way to the sensory level. At each level, you have billions of possible goals (reference perceptions) and at any given moment your awareness is focused on one of these possibilities. What we recognized was that people were setting new references, either by gaining new perceptions through learning or by shifting their focus to a different reference. In many instances, the shift was to a higher level. For example, from what do I want to do (program) to who do I want to be (principles). At other times it was from one reference to another reference at the same level, like the type of father Glenn wanted to be to the type of husband he wanted to be. Today all of the BE-Print for Living curriculums ask individuals to **SHIFT**, meaning shift your awareness. Thus far in this book we have asked you to become more consciously aware and to *shift* some beliefs and some principles; now we are asking you to *shift* some programs.

You may be familiar with SMART goals. **SMART** serves as a mnemonic device for goals that are **S**pecific, **M**easurable, **A**ttainable, **R**esults-oriented and **T**ime bound. The idea behind the acronym is to help you remember criteria for developing effective goals. The problem is that goals define a desired end result. *But we want you to work on becoming the person you have always wanted to be. That's a process that never ends.* We love the idea of making life simple, so we came up with our own mnemonic device: **SHIFT!**

The word SHIFT is both an acronym and a reminder of what you are trying to accomplish. The term captures the essence of developing new programs, procedures, routines, and rituals.

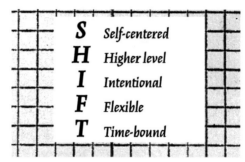

S   *Self-centered*
H   *Higher level*
I   *Intentional*
F   *Flexible*
T   *Time-bound*

Self-centered. Be sure that whatever procedure you develop is totally within your control. These procedures can involve others, but not be dependent upon them. Measuring your ability to be loving by hearing someone else say they love you is not in your control. What is within your control are the acts of kindness that you do for someone you love. As an example, you might write, "I will perform at least two acts of kindness towards my family members each day." Be careful not to expect a specific response from someone else. Effective procedures are unconditional, enacted without an expectation of recognition from others. (Remember this book is all about YOU!) *Your success can only be measured by your actions and intentions, not by the actions and intentions of others.* Responsible self-evaluation involves evaluating those things that are within your control. Here's an example: After viewing *Fireproof,* a movie that portrays the inspiring love story of a firefighter, his wife, and a marriage worth rescuing, Glenn decided to change one of his routines based on an idea from the movie. He began a journaling process where each day for forty days he entered a characteristic he cherished in his wife. He was quickly amazed at the difference within himself and the evidence within his marriage when he shifted his thinking and acted on it by changing a routine. Around day 15, he got stuck so he shifted his focus to a higher level and asked himself what type of a husband he wanted to be. He then completed a list of forty attributes that he appreciates in his wife, Kelli. Today he continues the practice, the only difference is he doesn't worry about duplicates. In fact, he recognizes that duplicates are indicators of what he finds most important in his relationship. Remember that it is irresponsible to evaluate yourself based on something you aren't responsible for. Keep it self-centered.

Higher level. When procedures are clearly linked to who you want to be and what you believe, you are more likely to persevere through the small setbacks along the way. Religious ceremonies and practices are some of the most deeply rooted programs individuals experience from a young age. Often the principle behind the practice is lost in its day-to-day practice. When rituals and ceremonies are carried out without being linked to higher levels of perception, they easily become meaningless and are viewed as obligations rather than opportunities. ***Effective practices must intentionally be linked to higher-level references, at the beliefs and principles level.*** One way to practice this is to continuously ask yourself, *When I do _____ what does it say about me and my character? When I do _____ what does it say about what I believe?* Another way to move toward higher levels is to begin creating *To Be* lists, rather than *To Do* lists.

When it comes to procedures, we also emphasize reaching higher so you continually stretch upward and reach beyond your limits. Cherie Carter-Scott, author of *Life Is a Game*, frames it this way: "Know your limits, not so that you can honor them, but so that you can smash them to pieces and reach for magnificence." When Shelley was growing through her divorce, many of her routines changed. In the midst of it all she went from walking a couple of times a week to exercising six days a week for a half an hour, plus walking, and a twice weekly Pilates class. When she started, it seemed beyond reach. But then she connected it to two higher-level principles: (1) to model for her sons healthy ways to deal with frustration and (2) to be healthier. Through the experience she learned that she is more successful when exercise is ritualistic in nature and when she is accountable to others. (This idea of outside accountability can be important as you think about developing new procedures. We will explore this concept later in the BE-Print series.) Make sure that the habit you are trying to develop is something you really want, not just something you *think* you should achieve because everyone else is doing it. You must make a strong emotional commitment to the change in order to really make the shift.

Intentional. Changing your routines doesn't happen by accident. Intentionality involves clearly declaring what you want. Shifting to something new requires purposeful, focused attention. The first thing you need to do is sit down somewhere quiet and really think about what you really want. The beliefs and principles you have already taken time to explore are the preparation for creating or changing your rituals and routines. Have you ever read the directions on a bottle of shampoo? They all pretty much read the same: "Apply shampoo to wet hair, gently massage. Rinse and repeat as necessary." Well, intentions need to be similarly applied. Intentions don't happen once, they need to be repeated as many times as necessary. When you are clear on your intentions, they point out where not to go and what not to do as much as they help you go where you want to go. Clear intentions lead to faster, clearer decisions that move you more quickly toward your dreams. **Write them, share them, act on them, and repeat as necessary.** Affirmations are a daily declaration of our intent, they reaffirm to ourselves and the world who we want to be. Create a few key affirmations to support your growth. The word *intention* derives from the Latin word *intentio*, which in turn derives from the verb *intendere*, which means being directed towards some goal. Clear, passionate intentions marshal your energy, amplifying them to the precision and strength of a laser beam directed at whatever you want to manifest in your life. In *The Intention Experiment*, Lynn McTaggart writes, "Targeting your thoughts — or what scientists ponderously refer to as 'intention' and 'intentionality' — appears to produce an energy potent enough to change physical reality. *A simple thought seems to have the power to change our world.*"

Swimmers, skaters, weightlifters, and basketball players all employ intention to enhance their levels of performance. Athletes of all varieties now routinely perform what is variously termed "mental rehearsals," "mental practice," "implicit practice," or "covert rehearsal." A mental rehearsal is a way to declare one's intent to win. Focused intention is now deemed essential for star athletes to improve their games. The movie *Cool Runnings*, based on the true story of the first Jamaican bobsled team trying to make it to the winter Olympics, features a scene of the athletes sitting in a bathtub running the course in their minds. Mental rehearsal is a good way to ready yourself for beginning a new routine and to test the power of your intentions. Intentions, declared to yourself and the world, rally the forces of the universe.

In our classes in the jail we ask participants each day to declare an intent for the day. We ask them to identify one key principle to focus on throughout the day. We ask them to write about it in a journal, and to end their day reflecting on their progress. It is a good reminder that every day we have is special. After all, you will only have one _____*(today's date)*_____ — you might as well make it memorable.

Flexible. One the most difficult parts of trying something new is sticking with it. This is often easier when what you are trying is *flexible* enough to accommodate the ever-changing environment. You also need to cut yourself some slack. Being flexible means continuous self-evaluation. Self-evaluation of your progress can be a real energy boost in trying on something new. Give yourself credit for any progress you are making — even small changes make big differences over time. Flexibility and self-evaluation along the way also allow you to make mid-course corrections. Maybe an unforeseen route has come into view, or you learned that you were too narrowly focused, or you recognized you needed to pause and take a time out to learn something new before continuing. You may find that your passion, values, principles, or beliefs have changed and the routines you are practicing need to change too. Glenn tells of his goal of running a marathon by the time he turned 55. Setting this goal when he was overweight and out of shape, he trained for two years, but fell short. He did not run a marathon, but during this time, he lost thirty pounds, ran more than twenty 5K races, a dozen 10K's, and one half marathon. He still exercises routinely, but the goal has changed from running a marathon to living a healthy life style. This is the essence of flexibility.

Time-bound. Of all the SHIFT criteria, this is the most difficult to explain because it is riddled with paradox. We want you be flexible with yourself and at the same time set deadlines and specify quantities. We want you to establish a number of days or a date for self-evaluating your progress, but we don't want you to focus on a specific number of days. That's OK, because exploring a paradox is a very powerful brain process. As the brain struggles to understand and resolve the paradox, creativity kicks in. Paradoxes involve two ideas that appear to be polar opposites, like "less is more" or "jumbo shrimp." But in some way, they make sense. The process of trying to resolve the paradox of forming *time-bound yet flexible* habits brings creativity into the process.

It has been said that new habits take at least twenty-one days to begin to become part of your system. Many businesses offer a thirty-day free trial. Many scriptures use the idea of forty days and forty nights when it comes to making major changes. Most processes within the human body happen in twenty-eight days. For instance, it takes twenty-eight days to replace the cells of a human being's epidermis completely. A women's menstrual cycle is twenty-eight days, the lining of the stomach and intestines are new every twenty-eight days. Dopamine-related (mood-related) habits take sixteen weeks to be fully changed. No matter what numbers you pick, the problem with focusing on a certain number of days is that you may tend to let your guard down once you reach the number. Not picking any numbers is even riskier. It's important to set realistic timelines for starting a new habit. Habits are simply repeated patterns, rituals, and routines that have become so much a part of you that you no longer recognize them. There is absolutely no magic number of days that you need to reach to make a new behavior a habit. Only you can answer the question, *How often and for how long are you willing to commit to trying on a new behavior?*

In the beginning, it is a lot easier to agree to try something for thirty days rather than to commit to it for a lifetime. People in alcohol and drug recovery make a commitment each and every day, one day at a time. As we mentioned with flexibility, the key to living the paradox is to learn to self-evaluate often. Setting a time frame is not meant to measure success or failure, but is a reminder to self-evaluate progress. We recommend self-evaluating daily to begin with. At the end or beginning of each day, evaluate your progress. Don't look only at what isn't working. Instead give yourself credit for even the smallest shifts. If you aren't sticking with it, ask yourself, *What am I doing instead?* This question will help you recognize where your energy is going. Maybe your target was unrealistic; move it a bit and make adjustments. If you keep moving the target, however, recognize that you are probably not committed and you need to reevaluate the whole program. Repeat as necessary.

When Shelley first started going to Curves, a gym for women designed around a half-hour workout, a big selling point was that it required only thirty minutes three times a week. After taking measurements every two weeks, it was a real energy boost to realize that every pound she lost was an inch off her body somewhere. Keeping track of these small incremental changes kept her going.

When you write out your new procedure, quantify it and set a deadline for having embedded it into your regular practices. Then keep it flexible. Think about which principle you really want to focus on. Write a statement that captures the change you want to make. Make sure your statement answers the following: "What would I accept as evidence that I am living this principle?" The evidence you choose will point to what program you will adopt. For example, if the principle is *Be wise*, the statement could be *Every forty days I will read a book related to a topic I'm interested in and want to know more about.*

Principle _____

■ *How I might measure my success. (What evidence would I accept that I am living by this principle?)*

■ *Which category (or categories) does the principle fit under: relationships, wealth, health, intellect, or spirituality?*

■ *How is it linked to any of your other top five principles?*

■ *If you change the procedure outlined in your statement, what belief will you be living?*

When you think about implementing your new behavior, are you excited? If not, go back and try again. You should be passionate about what you are trying to change or it is unlikely that you will follow through. Remember, this is an *opportunity*, not an *obligation*. If you don't see it that way, you still have more work to do.

Now, let's put it to the SHIFT test!

The **SHIFT** *Test*

S *How is it **specific**? How could it be totally within your control?*

H *How is it **higher-level**? How might you link it to one of your principles or beliefs?*

I *How is it **intentional**?*

F *How is it **flexible**?*

T *How is it **time-bound**?*

Instead of creating a whole new habit, you may want to tweak an already existing habit. You may already follow a diet that eliminates red meat. You may now wish to eat only fruits, grain, vegetables, eggs, and cheese. This approach is successful in changing habits for many people. You may want to get rid of a bad habit. Remember to shift the focus to grabbing something new, rather than giving something up. Focus on what you want, not on what you don't want. Becoming healthier replaces a lot of unhealthy habits. Instead of cutting out sweets, add more fruits and vegetables; instead of stopping drinking alcohol, focus on being clean and sober. We highly recommend that you think big and start small. *Take on one new change at a time... try it on and then evaluate how it's going.*

Now think about with whom you will share it. When Glenn begins work on a new behavior he is fond of asking someone close to him to act as an accountability buddy. He may not share his whole plan with others, but he will ask them to help him be accountable to the changes he is trying to make. He tells them specifically what he wants them to ask him and how often he wants them to ask. The buddy's job is to simply follow through and most importantly be non-judgmental of Glenn's progress.

With whom will you share your target?

If you plan to implement an accountability buddy be specific about how you want them to help, and how often you want them to help. One time Glenn asked Shelley to call him once a week and ask him "So how's the list coming?" Her job at that point was just to listen.

Now the most important step: **ACT ON IT!**

What will be the first action you take toward developing your new habit?

When you think about your life and how it will be different with this new behavior as an integral part of your daily living, are you *thrilled*? If not, rinse and repeat! Once you have created this new habit, it's time to take on your next challenge, maybe in a different area of your life. Come back often and keep revising.

What did you learn about your ability to develop habits?

■ *To your way of thinking how are procedures, rituals, and routines the same or different?*

■ *Where does skill come into the equation?*

You Are a Never-Ending Story

> " Life's biggest challenge is
> to discover your personal
> essence and then
> self-actualize."
>
> Brian E. Roscher

Change is the only constant in today's world. Every person on this planet is creating a personal journey that is constantly unfolding. Personally, we are both a work in progress with no end in sight. We have taken detours, gotten out of the water to wait out a storm or two, and changed our destination mid-stream many times. As we change, so does the BE-Print. What you have in your hands today will probably not be what we use tomorrow in our seminars. It has been a struggle to set on paper what we have been developing for the past five years. As of today, we have taught hundreds of classes in the jail, and each new class has meant a new set of materials. Each time we get into the water, something has changed. We want you to approach your BE-Print in the same way. Keep coming back and diving in. Continue to re-examine your beliefs to re-establish your five key principles. Re-form your agreements and redevelop your procedures, routines, rituals, and habits. Continue to live your life with meaning. As Chaim Potok said, "We must fill our lives with meaning; meaning is not automatically given to life." We believe that the hard work of diving deep and developing your BE-Print is worth it.

Each of you is a bundle of potentiality waiting to be ignited. The BE-Print is intended to help you discover the spark within that is uniquely you. Light it and let it burn in each and every moment of your life. Allow your brilliance to shine out to the world and provide light for others to see their way. We know from experience that those who develop and follow their BE-Print shine from within. They have a sense of dignity and calm that surrounds them even in the most difficult of moments. They look to themselves for happiness, for confirmation that they are on the right path. And they know that they are OK by themselves, but better with others. We believe this comes from each of them taking the time to explore and become the people they really want to be. Creating a BE-Print is not a magic bullet that will fix all problems; it is a guide to help you build the life you want and to face the challenges along the way. We can't swim for you, but we can coach you along the way and throw you a life preserver if you really need help.

In our next book in the BE-Print series, we will take a closer look at self-evaluation, self-discipline, and how to RE-Print your BE-Print. These processes act like support pillars helping you maintain the structure created in your BE-Print. In the meantime periodically practice self-evaluation by asking yourself, "How is what I am doing working?" Then quickly follow up with your next step. Each step along the way can be carried out safely when we are constantly monitoring the environmental changes and revising what we want. As you continue the BE-Print journey, we will swim into the depths of self-exploration by asking you to further explore your beliefs, principles, and procedures. In addition, we will share some hints on how to manage your emotions.

Our lives have been dedicated to changing the world. Like Gandhi, we believe that we need to be the changes we want to see in the world. One of the changes close to our hearts is to help people learn the essential life skill of self-evaluation.

We both are continuously revising and editing our personal BE-Prints. Please visit us often on our website and see how we are changing. Come join us for one of our upcoming seminars and look for our next BE-Print book as we continue our journey up stream together.

Bibliography

Adams, Kathleen. *Journal to the Self: Twenty-Two Paths to Personal Growth.* Warner Books, 1990.

Arntz, William, Betsy Chasse & Mark Vincente. *What tHe ßLeeP Do wE (k)πow!?.* Health Communications, Inc., 2005.

Boffey, Barnes. *My Gift in Return: Thoughts on the Journey to Becoming Real.* New View Publications, 2003.

Boffey, Barnes. *Reinventing Yourself: A Control Theory Approach to Becoming the Person You Want to Be.* New View, 1993.

Bridges, William. *Transitions: Making Sense of Life's Changes.* Addison-Wesley Publishing, 1990.

Brown, Les. *Live Your Dreams.* Harper Collins, 2001.

Butler-Bowdon, Tom. *50 Spiritual Classics: Timeless Wisdom from 50 Great Books of Inner Discovery, Enlightenment & Purpose.* MJF Books, 2005.

Byrne, Rhonda. *The Secret.* Atria Books, 2006.

Carey, Timothy A. *The Method of Levels: How to Do Psychotherapy Without Getting in the Way.* Living Control Systems Publishing, 2006.

Chaiklin, Seth. "The Zone of Proximal Development in Vygotsky's Analysis of Learning and Instruction." In Kozulin, A., Gindis, B., Ageyev, V., & Miller, S. (editors). *Vygotsky's Educational Theory and Practice in Cultural Context.* Cambridge University Press, 2003.

Chaline, Eric. *The Book of Zen: The Path to Inner Peace.* Barron's Educational Series, 2003.

Coelho, Paulo. *The Valkyries.* HarperCollins, 1998.

Covey, Stephen R. *The Seven Habits of Highly Effective People.* Simon and Schuster, 1989.

Dyer, Wayne. *The Power of Intention.* Hay House, 2004.

Gladwell, Malcolm. *The Tipping Point: How Little Things Can Make a Big Difference.* Little, Brown & Co., 2000.

Gladwell, Malcolm, *Blink: The Power of Thinking Without Thinking.* Little, Brown & Co., 2000.

Good, E. Perry, Jeff Grumley, and Shelley Roy. *A Connected School.* New View Publications, 2003.

Greenfield, Susan A. *The Human Brain: A Guided Tour.* Basic Books, 1997.

Hanh, Thich Naht. *The Art of Mindful Living: How to Bring Love, Compassion, and Inner Peace into Your Daily Life.* Sounds True, 2000.

Hanh, Thich Naht. *Peace is Every Step: The Path of Mindfulness in Everyday Life.* Bantam Books, 1992.

Hardy, Kerry D. *These Four Walls.* Xulon Press, 2009.

Hay, Louise L. *You Can Heal Your Life.* Hay House, 2006.

Hicks, Esther, and Jerry Hicks. *The Amazing Power of Deliberate Intent: Living the Art of Allowing.* Hay House, 2006.

Johnson, Spence. *The Present: The Secret to Enjoying Your Work And Life, Now!* Doubleday, 2003.

Johnson, Spence. *Who Moved My Cheese: An Amazing Way to Deal with Change in Your Work and in Your Life.* Penguin Putnam, 2002.

Kuhn, Thomas S. *The Structure of Scientific Revolutions.* University of Chicago Press, 1962.

McGraw, Phil. *Life Strategies: Doing What Works, Doing What Matters.* Hyperion Books, 1999.

McTaggart, Lynne. *The Intention Experiment: Using Your Thoughts to Change Your Life and the World.* Free Press, 2007.

Moss Kanter, Rosabeth. *The Change Masters: Innovation & Entrepreneurship in the American Corporation.* Simon & Schuster, 1983.

Powers, William T. *Behavior: The Control of Perception.* Aldine, 1973.

Powers, William T. *Making Sense of Behavior.* Benchmark Publications, 1998.

Powers, William T. *Living Control Systems: Selected Papers of William T. Powers.* The Control System Group, 1989.

Powers, William T., and Richard J. Robertson. *Introduction to Modern Psychology: The Control Theory View.* The Control System Group, 1990.

Radin, Dean. *Entangled Minds: Extrasensory Experiences in a Quantum Reality.* Paraview, 2006.

Roy, Shelley. *A People Primer: The Nature of Living Systems.* New View Publications, 2008.

Ruiz, Don Miguel. *The Four Agreements: A Practical Guide to Personal Freedom.* Amber-Allen Publishing, 1997.

Senge, Peter, Richard Boss, Bryan Smith, Charlotte Roberts, and Art Leiner. *The Fifth Discipline Fieldbook.* Doubleday Dell Publishing Group, 1994.

Smith, Glenn, and Melanie Conger. *Schools with Character: Creating the School We Want and Becoming the Person I Really Want to Be.* Journal Jots Publishing, 2002.

Vanderijt, Hetty, and Frans Plooij. *The Wonder Weeks: How to Turn Your Baby's 8 Great Fussy Phases into Magical Leaps Forward.* Rodale, 2003.

Walsch, Neale Donald. *Conversations with God: An Uncommon Dialogue (Book I).* G.P. Putnam's Sons, 1996.

———. *Conversations with God: An Uncommon Dialogue (Book II).* Hampton Roads Publishing, 1997.

———. *Conversations with God: An Uncommon Dialogue (Book III).* Hampton Roads Publishing, 1998.

BE-Print for Living, Inc.

BE-Print for Living, Inc., was founded in 2009 by Shelley Roy and Glenn Smith. Shelley and Glenn developed the original BE-Print, along with business partners George Hallak and Andre Cox, to offer service providers a standardized and comprehensive science-based approach to helping others help themselves. All BE-Print products are based on the latest scientific research on human behavior, the learning brain, change management, and leadership. We offer direct service, consultation, coaching and customized curriculum development for individuals, mental health providers, schools, families, religious organizations, businesses, and other organizations.

For more information about how to bring the concepts described in this book to your area, business, or organization call us at 866.858.5433. Customized training is available in the form of a one-day overview, a three-day seminar, or year-long experience. We have programs designed for individuals young and old; educators and students; parents and children; management and employees; correctional officers and adjudicated juveniles and adults; coaches and their players, along with leaders and their constituents. We invite you to attend one of our regularly scheduled seminars, held yearly in October and March in Charlotte, North Carolina. For more information, visit us on the web at www.be-print.net.

866.858.5433 ■ WWW.BE-PRINT.NET

113

Shelley A.W. Roy is CEO of BE-Print for Living, Inc., president of Synergy Transition Consulting, president of Five Crows Publishing, and founding member and senior faculty member of the International Association for Applied Control Theory. A recognized leader in human resource development, Shelley, has worked with thousands of adults in a wide range of learning situations. For more than ten years she provided facilitation to over seventy improvement teams and several multi-agency collaboratives. She has taught in the K-12 school system and at the university level, in West Berlin, Germany; the Navajo Reservation, Tohatchi, New Mexico; Junction City, Kansas; Leigh, Nebraska; St. Cloud, Minnesota; and Charlotte, North Carolina. In her workshops and seminars across the United States and internationally, she shares the latest in leadership, human behavior, effective communication, brain compatible instruction, change management, and team building. Shelley has written *Freshman Orientation: Avoid the Dangers of Destructive Decision Making* (Xulon Press, 2009) with co-author K.D. Hardy, *A People Primer: The Nature of Living Systems* (New View Publications, 2008), and *A Connected School* (New View Publications, 2003) with co-authors E. Perry Good and Jeff Grumley. For more information about her or to read her blog visit her on the web at www.shelleyawroy.com.

A portion of **Shelley's BE-Print: My Personal Agreement**

My mission is to model compassion and caring towards all living and non-living things. To help others recognize the gifts they have to offer and encourage them to give these gifts to the world. To be a passionate teacher who helps individuals take their next step in learning.

Glenn M. Smith is president of Be-Print for Living, Inc. He started his career in 1973, when he founded and directed the first community-based group home for youth ever established in West Virginia. After conducting his graduate studies at Cornell University in 1980, Glenn studied with the Institute for Reality Therapy under William Glasser and in 1987 became a Faculty Member.

Since that time, Glenn became associated with William Powers, founder of the Control Systems Group and Perceptual Control Theory a scientific model that explains the nature of living systems. In 1998 Glenn helped organize and develop the International Association of Applied Control Theory, in which he also serves as a Senior Faculty Member.

Glenn is a gifted counselor, life coach, and strategist. As a skilled mediator, trainer, and consultant, he has provided coaching to counselors, educators, business managers, and all types of organizations throughout the United States and internationally. He is the founder of Life Connections, Inc., a private counseling and professional coaching organization near Charlotte, North Carolina. Life Connections also serves as a BE-Print provider. Glenn has co-authored the books *Quality Times for Quality Kids* and *Schools With Character*. He lives in the Charlotte area with his wife, Kelli, and his teenage children, Karlie and Mattson.

A portion of **Glenn's BE-Print: Relationships**

I believe that relationships are life's grandest opportunity to discover who you really are. When I am with another person I can self-evaluate who I am and who I am not. Relationships also give me the opportunity to learn and to grow, to challenge my beliefs, my view of myself, and my view of the world. I believe that I am OK alone, but I am better with others.

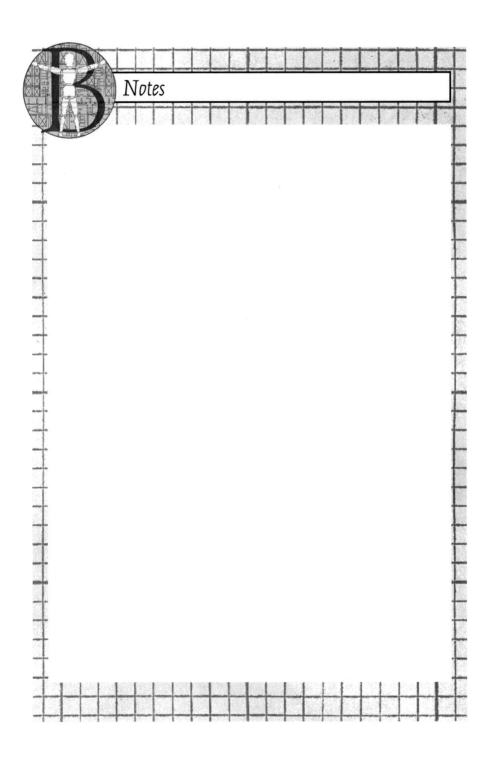

Notes

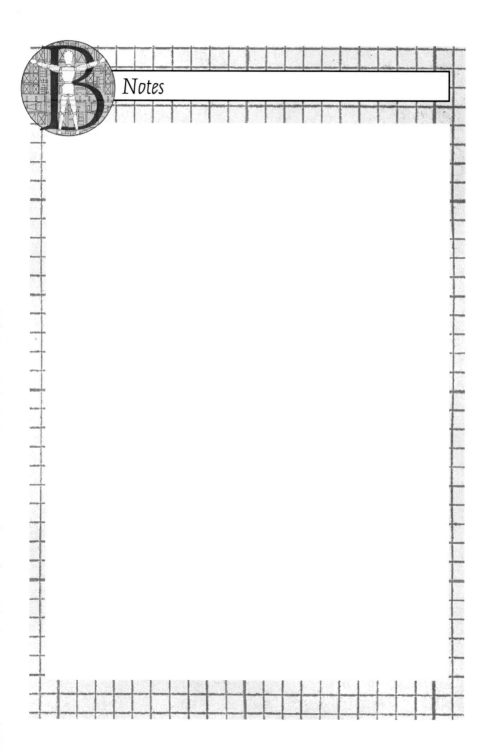

Notes

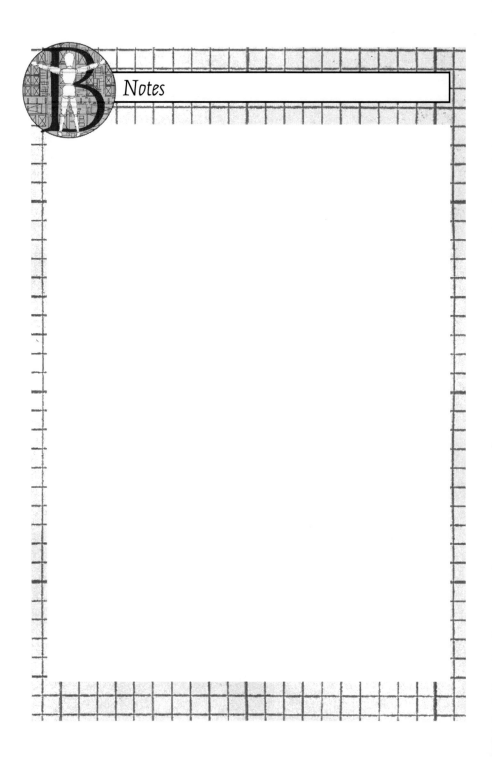

Notes

CPSIA information can be obtained at www.ICGtesting.com
Printed in the USA
BVOW041858171011

273858BV00001B/12/P

9 780984 431403